IN THE
MEANTIME

In the Meantime Study Guide
© 2017 North Point Ministries, Inc.

Italics in Scripture quotations are the author's emphasis.
Unless otherwise indicated, Scripture quotations are from:
The Holy Bible, New International Version (NIV)
© 1973, 1978, 1984, 2011 by Biblica, Inc.™
Used by permission. All rights reserved worldwide.

Printed in Canada.
ALL RIGHTS RESERVED.

No part of this publication may be reproduced, stored in a retrieval system, or transmitted in any form or by any means—electronic, mechanical, photocopying, recording, or otherwise—without prior written permission.

Cover design by North Point Media
Interior design by Pat Malone

IN THE MEANTIME

Study Guide

LEADER INFO	**4**
HOW TO USE THIS STUDY	**5**
PART 1:	**6**
PART 2:	**12**
PART 3:	**18**
PART 4:	**24**
PART 5:	**30**
PART 6:	**36**

Here are some ideas to get you started.

LEADERS:

Need some help? It's okay. We all do.

A full walk-through of the study guide with notes on how to navigate each session is available at **groupleaders.org/inthemeantime.**

VIDEOS:

The video sessions that complement this study can be found on the:

- **Anthology Mobile App** (free on the Apple App Store and Google Play)
- *In The Meantime* **DVD** (available on Amazon)

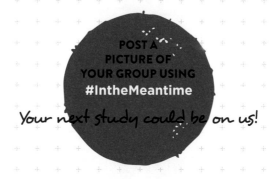

POST A PICTURE OF YOUR GROUP USING #IntheMeantime

Your next study could be on us!

DURING A GROUP MEETING

1. HANG OUT.
(about 30 minutes)

Our lives move so fast these days. Take some time to talk about what's going on in the lives of those in your group. Asking about things like job interviews, the health of their kids, and how their weeks are going goes a long way in building community.

2. WATCH THE VIDEO AND DOODLE ALONG.
(about 20 minutes)

When we designed this study guide, we had note-taking in mind. So while you're watching the video, take advantage of the extra space and grid pages for notes and/or drawings, depending on your note-taking style.

3. DISCUSS AND COMPLETE THE ACTIVITIES.
(about 45 minutes)

Depending on the session, your group will have Discussion Questions and scenarios to think through, as well as activities to do. Putting pen to paper can give you deeper insight into the content.

4. PRAY.
(about 5 minutes)

Keep it simple and real. Use the prayer provided. Ask God to help you apply what you've learned that week.

PART 1:
The New Normal

VIDEO RECAP

JOHN THE BAPTIZER

> "Truly I tell you, among those born of women there has not risen anyone **greater** than John the Baptist..."
>
> (Matthew 11:11)

> When Jesus heard that John had been put in prison, he **withdrew** to Galilee. Leaving Nazareth, he went and **lived** in Capernaum...
>
> (Matthew 4:12–13)

> "Blessed is anyone who does not **stumble** on account of me."
>
> (Matthew 11:6)

Don't interpret God's _____ as _____.

LAZARUS

*"Lord, the one you **love** is sick." Now Jesus **loved** Martha and her sister and Lazarus. So when he heard that Lazarus was sick, **he stayed where he was** two more days.*

(John 11:3, 5–6)

Don't confuse God's apparent **absence** for _____.

Answer Key for Blanks

silence   apathy
absence

IN THE MEANTIME

LET'S TALK ABOUT IT

1 During the message, Andy stated that people often interpret God's silence as absence. Why do you think people do that?

2 How have you seen someone demonstrate great faith in God despite difficult circumstances?

3 Read Matthew 4:12–13 and answer the question that follows the verse.

When Jesus heard that John had been put in prison, he withdrew to Galilee. Leaving Nazareth, he went and lived in Capernaum...

When have you felt like God was "at the beach" while you were "in the desert"?

PART 1

Notes

4 Which of these statements best describes your relationship with God while you were "in the desert"?

☐ God was absent from my life.
☐ God was apathetic to what I was going through.
☐ God must be angry with me.
☐ God must have a purpose for me in this trial.

5 Your unanswered prayer doesn't mean that God is uninterested. Is there something you are wrestling with today and wondering when or if God is going to show up? Share with the group.

THIS WEEK, THINK ABOUT...

Jesus loved John the Baptizer and Lazarus. Yet he didn't respond in ways we would expect. How do these two stories make you rethink God's silence or apparent absence in your own life?

PRAYER

"Heavenly Father, remind me in my *in-the-meantime* moments that you are not absent or apathetic. Teach me to replace these lies with the truth of how much you really do love me."

YOUR *unanswered* PRAYER DOES NOT MEAN THAT GOD IS *uninterested.*

POST A PICTURE OF YOUR GROUP USING #IntheMeantime

Your next study could be on us!

PART 2:
A Purpose and a Promise

VIDEO RECAP

*Therefore, **in order to** keep me from becoming conceited, I was **given** a **thorn** in my flesh, a messenger of Satan, to **torment** me.*

(2 Corinthians 12:7)

- Painful
- Humiliating
- Debilitating

*Three times I _____ with the Lord to take it away from me. But he **said** to me, "My **grace** is sufficient for you, for my **power** is made perfect in weakness."*

(2 Corinthians 12:8–9)

- **Permanent**

*Therefore I will _____ all the more gladly about my weaknesses, **so that** Christ's power may rest on me.*

(2 Corinthians 12:9)

Embracing your _____ is a prerequisite to experiencing Christ's _____.

*That is why, for Christ's sake, I delight in weaknesses, in insults, in hardships, in persecutions, in difficulties. For when I am **weak**, then I am **strong**.*

(2 Corinthians 12:10)

Answer Key for Blanks

pleaded	inability
boast	ability

LET'S TALK ABOUT IT

1 Why do you think people assume that faith in God will remove adversity from their lives? Have you ever made that assumption?

2 Why is it difficult to accept that challenging circumstances can come from a loving God?

3 Do you feel permission to plead with God to take away your difficult circumstances? How do you believe he responds to that kind of prayer?

4 Has there ever been a time that God told you no?

PART 2

Notes

5 Read 2 Corinthians 12:7–10 and complete the activity that follows.

Therefore, in order to keep me from becoming conceited, I was given a thorn in my flesh, a messenger of Satan, to torment me. Three times I pleaded with the Lord to take it away from me. But he said to me, "My grace is sufficient for you, for my power is made perfect in weakness." Therefore I will boast all the more gladly about my weaknesses, so that Christ's power may rest on me. That is why, for Christ's sake, I delight in weaknesses, in insults, in hardships, in persecutions, in difficulties. For when I am weak, then I am strong.

Take a moment to write down what is or has been a "thorn in your flesh." What can you do to begin to view that "thorn" as a gift that comes with a purpose and a promise? If you are comfortable, share with the group.

6 In the message, Andy said, "You are either in the middle of, have just gone through, or are about to go through an *in-the-meantime* season of life." How does that statement make you feel?

THIS WEEK, THINK ABOUT...

Andy said, "Embracing your inability is a prerequisite to experiencing Christ's ability." Think of an "inability" or a "thorn" in your life, then use the grief continuum below to evaluate where you are. What can you do this week to move a step closer to acceptance?

Denial	Anger	Depression	Bargaining	Acceptance

PRAYER

"Heavenly Father, teach me how to live in my weaknesses so I may learn to depend on Jesus. Remind me that it is in my weaknesses that Christ's strength and ability are on display."

EMBRACING *your inability* IS A PREREQUISITE TO *experiencing* CHRIST'S ABILITY.

Video Notes

PART 3:
Yes, You Can

VIDEO RECAP

While imprisoned in Rome, Paul uses his *"in-the-meantime"* moment to write letters to his fellow Christians in Ephesus, Colossae, and Philippi. The books, known as the Prison Epistles, were extremely influential in shaping the growth of Christianity.

Paul had no idea what hung in the balance of his decision to remain faithful when remaining faithful was difficult.

You have no idea **what** or **who** hangs in the balance of your decision to remain faithful when everything around you says to be faithless.

It's often in the context of **adversity** that God does his most amazing things in us and through us.

CONTENTMENT

I rejoiced greatly in the Lord that at last you **renewed your concern** *for me. Indeed, you were concerned, but you had no opportunity to show it. I am not saying this because I am in need, for I have _____ to be*

_____ *whatever the* **circumstances**. *I* **know** *what it is to be in need, and I* **know** *what it is to have plenty. I have* **learned the secret** *of being content in any and* _____ _____, *whether well fed or hungry, whether living in plenty or in want. I can* **do** *all this through* **him** *who* **gives** *me [***his***] strength.*

(Philippians 4:10–13)

Contentment: to be okay on the **inside** when the **outside** is not okay

The **life**, **strength**, and **endurance** of Jesus is available to us in Christ.

Answer Key for Blanks

learned   every situation

content

IN THE MEANTIME

LET'S TALK ABOUT IT

1 Do you know someone who lives with discontentment? How does it affect the quality of his or her life?

2 In the message, Andy said, "You have no idea what or who hangs in the balance of your decision to remain faithful when everything around you says 'Be faithless.'" Do you have a personal example of how remaining faithful turned out?

3 Take a moment to reflect on your own season(s) of adversity. Share one or two sentences about your experience.

4 In the midst of adversity, we have a choice between being faithful and being faithless—which can be a feeling or in some cases a behavior. What does being faithless tend to look like for you personally?

☐ Hopelessness
☐ Fleeing
☐ Medicating
☐ Drinking
☐ Distractions
☐ Work

PART 3

Notes

☐ Spending
☐ TV, Video Games
☐ Avoidance
☐ Resentment
☐ Denial
☐ Other

5 Think back to the adversity example you noted above in Question 3. Was your response faithful? Faithless? A little of both?

6 What is your primary source of discontentment right now?

THIS WEEK, THINK ABOUT...

You can't, but Jesus can. You can be confident that he can because he dragged his own cross to a hill and died for your sin. Anyone who can do that on purpose can strengthen you when you're at your weakest. You can do all things through Christ who strengthens you.

PRAYER

God, I can't, but you can. Teach me the mystery of Christ in me.

YOU HAVE *no idea* WHAT HANGS IN THE BALANCE OF *your* RESPONSE TO YOUR IN-THE-MEANTIME *season.*

POST A PICTURE OF YOUR GROUP USING #IntheMeantime

Your next study could be on us!

PART 4:
(Andy Jones)
Where's Your Focus?

VIDEO RECAP

In the Meantime

I'll never be **happy** again.

Nothing **good** can come from this.

There's no **point** in continuing.

> As he went along, he saw a man blind from birth. His disciples asked him, "Rabbi, _____ _____, this man or his parents, that he was born blind?" "_____ this man nor his parents sinned," said Jesus, "but this happened so that the works of God might be **displayed** in him."
>
> (John 9:1-3)

When you focus on what's _____, you lose sight of what God makes _____.

Answer Key for Blanks

who sinned   wrong
Neither   right

IN THE MEANTIME

LET'S TALK ABOUT IT

1 Why is it tempting for people in the midst of difficult circumstances to compare their lives to the lives of others?

2 Read John 9:1–3 in the Part 4 Video Recap. The disciples were looking to attribute blame for the man's blindness. Why do we look to assign blame as a response to difficult circumstances?

3 During the message, Andy Jones said, "When you focus on what's wrong, you lose sight of what God makes right." Using the table on page 27, take two minutes and list what's not going well right now. Then, turn your focus to what God is making right.

4 As you consider your current circumstances, what is one thing you can do to begin to focus less on what's going wrong and more on what God is making right?

PART 4

	THINGS NOT GOING WELL	THINGS TO BE GRATEFUL FOR
Family		
Work		
Health		
Other		

THIS WEEK, THINK ABOUT...

As long as you're focused on what went wrong, you'll lose sight of what God is making right. This week, as you find your attention drifting in the direction of what is currently wrong, press reset—and remember that God is on display in your circumstances.

PRAYER

God, help me see how you are on display in my circumstances. Help me focus on what you have made right instead of what's wrong.

WHEN YOU FOCUS ON *what's wrong,* YOU LOSE SIGHT OF WHAT *God* MAKES *right.*

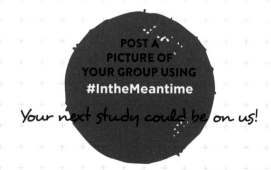

POST A PICTURE OF YOUR GROUP USING #IntheMeantime

Your next study could be on us!

Video Notes

PART 5:
Believe It or Not

VIDEO RECAP

*James, a servant of God and of the Lord Jesus Christ...**Consider** it pure **joy**, my brothers and sisters, whenever you **face** trials of many kinds, because you know that the **testing** of your **faith**...*

(James 1:1–3)

_____ test our _____ in God.

*You know that the **testing** of your **faith** produces **perseverance**.*

(James 1:3)

Trials produce _____ **faith**.

***Let** perseverance **finish** its work so that you may be **mature** and **complete**, not **lacking** anything.*

(James 1:4)

Let perseverance _____ its work so you will be **complete**.

Spiritual maturity is measured in terms of **persevering faith**, not **perfect behavior**.

> *If any of you lacks **wisdom**, you should ask God, who gives generously to all without finding fault, and it will be **given** to you.*
>
> (James 1:5)

Wisdom: the ability to see **current** circumstances within a **broader** context.

Video Notes

Answer Key for Blanks

Trails	persevering
confidence	complete

POST A PICTURE OF YOUR GROUP USING #IntheMeantime

Your next study could be on us!

IN THE MEANTIME

LET'S TALK ABOUT IT

1 Is there a situation or circumstance you wish you would have persevered through instead of hitting the eject button? Take a moment to reflect.

2 During the message, Andy said, "Faith that gets a yes from God is nothing compared to faith that gets no answer or no for an answer but endures anyway." How do you feel when you see people persevering through trials? Are you okay with the "no" or with no answer?

3 Read James 1:2-4 in the Part 5 Video Recap. How realistic is it to be able to consider your trials "pure joy"? Be honest.

4 James 1:5 says, *"If any of you lacks wisdom, you should ask God, who gives generously to all without finding fault, and it will be given to you."*

God responds to our requests for wisdom in different ways. Waiting only for "a sign" or an audible voice from God may mean missing out on the cues God is giving you.

Listed below are a few different ways God can respond to our requests for wisdom. Check the situations that are most relevant in your story. Add any others that might be missing and share with the group.

PART 5

Finding Wisdom In:

- Private Disciplines: quiet time, reading the Bible, prayer

  _____
  _____
  _____

- Providential Relationships: certain people in your life that are uniquely qualified to offer wise counsel

  _____
  _____
  _____

- Practical Teaching: messages, books, podcasts

  _____
  _____
  _____

- Personal Ministry: volunteering on Sunday, serving with a local nonprofit, mission trips

  _____
  _____
  _____

5 What came to mind when Andy said, "Spiritual maturity is measured in terms of persevering faith, not perfect behavior"?

Notes

THIS WEEK, THINK ABOUT...

Challenge the way you've thought about your trials. When you're living *in-the-meantime*, believe that God is at work in you to mature you and that we are perfected through perseverance.

PRAYER

"Heavenly Father: help me to consider my trials as 'pure joy' and to trust you in my *in-the-meantime* moments. Open my eyes this week to the wisdom you have for me."

WE ARE *perfected* THROUGH *perseverance.*

POST A PICTURE OF YOUR GROUP USING #IntheMeantime

Your next study could be on us!

PART 6:
Comfort Zone

VIDEO RECAP

*Praise be to the God and Father of our Lord Jesus Christ, the **Father** of **compassion** and the God of all **comfort**, who **comforts** us in **all** our troubles, **so that** we **can** comfort those in **any** trouble **with** the comfort we ourselves receive **from** God.*

(2 Corinthians 1:3-4)

God comforts _____ to comfort _____.

God comforts **us** through **others** to comfort **others**.

*For just as we share **abundantly** in the sufferings of Christ, **so also** our comfort **abounds** through Christ.*

(2 Corinthians 1:5)

Our _____ to comfort is determined by the _____ to which we've suffered.

> *If we are **distressed**, it is for **your** comfort and salvation; if **we** are comforted, it is for **your** comfort, which produces in you **patient endurance** of the same sufferings we suffer. And our hope for you is firm, because we know that just as you share in our **sufferings**, so also you share in our **comfort**.*
>
> (2 Corinthians 1:6–7)

Answer Key for Blanks

us	capacity
others	degree

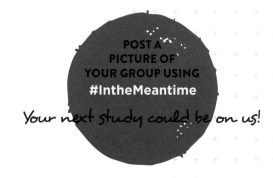

POST A PICTURE OF YOUR GROUP USING #IntheMeantime

Your next study could be on us!

IN THE MEANTIME

LET'S TALK ABOUT IT

1. When was a time when someone who had experienced circumstances similar to yours attempted to comfort you? Was it helpful?

2. Read 2 Corinthians 1:3–7 in the Part 6 Video Recap. In the midst of his own suffering, Paul is able to praise God for his compassion and comfort. Does this seem possible?

3. Have you ever had the opportunity to comfort someone because you've experienced a similar trial?

4. Giving and receiving comfort can be intensely emotional. Considering your answers for Questions 1 and 3, use the Feeling Wheel listed on page 39 to identify one word to describe how you felt in those situations. Share with the group.

5. During the message, Andy said, "Our capacity to comfort is determined by the degree to which we've suffered." Respond to that statement. In what ways is it hopeful? In what ways is it scary?

6. Does your *in-the-meantime* moment have to be fully resolved before you can comfort others?

PART 6

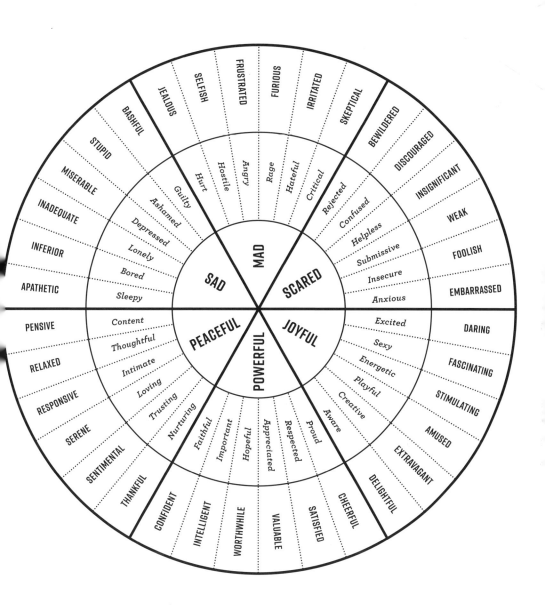

Feeling Wheel
Developed by Dr. Gloria Willcox

THIS WEEK, THINK ABOUT...

Make the most of your *in-the-meantime* moments. Comfort those who need comforting with the comfort you have received from God. Don't bury your sorrows. Leverage them for the sake of other people that you are uniquely qualified to comfort because you've been there, you understand, and you know there's life on the other side.

PRAYER

"Father, help me make the most of my *in-the-meantime* moments. Help me see the opportunities to leverage my story for someone else's benefit."

In the Meantime:

YOU *can* BE HAPPY AGAIN.

SOMETHING GOOD *can* COME FROM THIS.

THERE *is* A REASON TO CONTINUE LIVING.

POST A PICTURE OF YOUR GROUP USING #IntheMeantime

Your next study could be on us!